Meeting CHRIST at BROADWAY & BETHLEHEM

Day by Day Through Advent

Edward Hays

Forest of Peace   Notre Dame, Indiana

Founded in 1865, Ave Maria Press is a ministry of the Indiana Province of Holy Cross.

www.forestofpeace.com

ISBN-10 0-939516-84-5   ISBN-13 978-0-939516-84-1

Cover image ©2009 Edward M. Hays.

Cover and text design by Brian C. Conley.

Printed and bound in the United States of America.

PREFACE

This booklet is a manual of daily reflections, practices, and prayers for Advent sojourners who are challenged to live these days anticipating the coming of Emmanuel while living in a world already decorated for and celebrating Christmas. The Feast of the Nativity commemorates the birth of Jesus in Bethlehem and the coming of Emmanuel, "God-among-us," the Word-made-flesh. In preparation for that great feast, Advent begins by calling out to us, "Come, enter into these four weeks of preparation with prayer, repentance, and quiet contemplation." And at the very same time, the rest of the world calls to us even more loudly, "Come, join the party! Celebrate Christmas early with tinseled trees, the music of carols, and extravagant merry-making!"

Living in such a society makes having an authentic Advent seem almost impossible, yet "with God all things are possible." Not only is a holy Advent possible, but this season holds the lifetime adventure to which every disciple of Jesus is called. Enter then into a prayerful and thoughtful Advent because hidden within it is the holy mystery of yearning for the coming of the reign of God-among-us, while at the same time reveling in the joyful reality of that Kingdom already present here and now in our everyday lives.

Mindful that a mystic is simply one who experiences God, as you begin this Advent my wish for you is "May you have a merry, mystical Christmas—today and every day."

Edward Hays

First Sunday of Advent

Advent begins today at the intersection of Broadway and Bethlehem. The Incarnation—God enfleshed in Jesus and in each of us—that we celebrate on Christmas Day has already arrived at this busy crossroads. Today our Broadways and Main Streets, aglow with glitzy yuletide glamour and decorated in tinsel-lighted Christmas trees, exist side by side with silent Advent wreaths and the deep longing of yet-to-be-fulfilled promises. At the intersection of Broadway and Bethlehem we hear joyous carols along with our ageless plaintive songs crying for Emmanuel. Advent's "Now is the time to repent, fast, and amend our ways" has a head-on collision with the carols of angels singing, "Joy to the world, the Lord is come!"

As an Advent sojourner, you start out today on a four-week journey with one foot in each of these two seemingly contradictory worlds: one longing for Christ's coming and the other already joyously celebrating its arrival. For many, of course, Christmas is not really about Christ at all anymore, but is a loosely defined celebration of family ties, love, and general good will. These are not bad things to celebrate, of course, but fall far short of the meaning and mandates of the Christian feast.

Practicing Advent Joy

Embrace the tension of the Advent cross—as you are pulled in two opposite directions—one preparing for the coming of Christ and the other already rejoicing in his arrival.

O God of Our Longing,
Teach me how to enjoy the colorful carnival of Christmas
while yearning for the coming of Emmanuel the Liberator.

First Monday of Advent

The daily reflections in this booklet are intended to be read one each day. As with prescription medicine, don't overdose by reading ahead—swallowing a couple of days at once. One a day is sufficient, if taken properly. We are often instructed to take medications with a full glass of water. These reflections should be taken with a full dose of quiet. Set aside at least ten minutes each day to read, contemplate, and pray with them.

Yesterday, Sunday's church environment spoke loudly and clearly of Advent. Today the environment at work or school and certainly at the mall will likely be devoid of any trace of Advent. You will travel around a city or town decorated with Christmas trees and yuletide wreaths. Don't try to ignore them, but instead let these decorations sing to you, "Celebrate the Christmas birth of the Prince of Peace today by being more pleasant, patient, and non-judgmental." The heart of Christmas is God's enfleshment in Jesus, in us, and in all creation—an astonishing reality that is with us all year long!

Practicing Advent Joy

At work, social or civic events, and at home, the wisest way to spend these Advent days is to be as fully conscious as possible of the astoundingly unbelievable heart of Christmas—God's enfleshment in the world.

God of Clear Vision,
May I let this Advent meditation be eye medicine
so that I may see your presence in all I encounter.

An excellent daily Advent prayer comes from Pierre Teilhard de Chardin, the French Jesuit priest and scholar:

> Lord, grant that I may see, that I may see you,
> that I may see and feel your presence
> in all things and animating all things.

I encourage you to learn this by heart. Being brief, it can easily be used frequently throughout this day and in the coming days of Advent. The power of this prayer is that along with striving to see God in all things, it asks for the grace to "feel" Divine Mystery's energetic presence in all you touch.

"*All*," you ask? "Do you mean like touching the keys of my computer or the handle of the soup pot, and even petting my cat?"

Yes, the energetic heart of Christmas is at your fingertips in the abiding, enfleshed presence of God in all things. While people speak of experiencing the divine in a splendid sunset over the ocean or at the birth of a child, Advent calls you to experience that same divine presence in every event of life.

Practicing Advent Joy

This small Advent prayer will help you **see and feel** God "animating all things." Then by holding your cell phone, stroking your pets, and even holding the handle of your kitchen pot, your fingertips will joyfully feel "Christmas! The Divine Presence."

Awaken me to the touch of Christmas
as I feel you, my God,
throbbing with life in everything.

These four weeks of Advent are not simply a prayerful preparation for Christmas, but a four-week training course on how to live Christmas every day of the year. To live a yearlong Christmas requires consciously being a resident in a world enfleshed by God. To achieve this, go on an Advent vision quest. In earlier centuries, Native Americans went off as seekers on a vision quest involving solitude, fasting, and prayer. In the midst of it, the Great Spirit granted the seekers a vision of their true identity and their life path. They would then return to their people to live out their vision.

Jesus, after his baptism, went on the first Advent vision quest by entering the desert in solitude, seeking God. In his quest he was given a vision of his personal intimate oneness with God; then he, too, returned to his people to live out his vision. On this, your Advent vision quest, you are to see the same vision that he saw, and then with faith live it.

Practicing Advent Joy

The success of your Advent can be measured by your belief and awareness of God's presence in yourself, in others, and all things. When your Advent quest ends on Christmas Day, you will return to your family and community living that awesome Vision of Visions, enfleshed in you.

May my eyes ache, O God, to see a vision of you
in my mirror, in the faces of others, and in creation.

First Thursday of Advent

A common complaint this time of year is, "Christmas comes earlier each year! Stores are now decorated for the holidays just after Halloween!" However, Advent sojourners, who comprehend the heart of Christmas as the enfleshment of God in all life, respond, "Sadly, it doesn't come early enough or last longer!" The more awesome a sacred mystery, the more reminders we need of it so as not to lose our awareness and appreciation of it.

In this holiday season, images of Bethlehem's humble stable—the birthplace of Emmanuel (God among us)—abound. The cornerstone of Christmas and Christianity is God taking on human flesh in Jesus, but that wasn't the very first Incarnation. The first Bethlehem was fourteen billion years ago at the awe-inspiring fiery birth of the universe, where God became enfleshed in all created matter. So at that galactic Bethlehem, like any artist who empties herself into her masterpiece, God did the same. God emptied himself into the exploding universe of the hundreds of billions of galaxies and their planets—thus making it the first Incarnation. The Creator lovingly spoke on that Cosmic Christmas, and the Word became stars and galaxies, suns and moons, oceans and earth, fin, feather, and fleshy tissue.

Practicing Advent Joy

Venture outside today—perhaps at evening—and soak up the majesty of God all around you.

May I ever be aware that I'm living in that Cosmic Bethlehem, so to see with wonder all living things, all creation, and myself.

The Advent classic, "O Come, O Come, Emmanuel," cries out our ancient thirst for a liberator like a cracked, parched earth wailing for rain. Its melody and lyrics capture the ageless yearning of an oppressed people for a Messiah to come and set them free. As Christians we believe in the Incarnation, that God lived among us as a human person, Jesus of Nazareth, and continues to dwell with us as the risen Christ. So the lyrics might be changed to, "Rise up, rise up, Emmanuel, from within each of us!" Has Christ come, or are we still waiting?

Beliefs are strange things, capable of inhabiting heads but not hearts. If we believe with all our hearts that we are infused with the presence of our liberator God, why do we cry out to be set free? If the power of the Divine is within us, what human power on earth can hold us captive?

Perhaps we are Advent half-believers who should rather sing, "O come, Emmanuel, and rescue me from my unbelief." While it is admirable to pray and then patiently wait for God to come to save your troubled marriage or rescue you from temptation, is that how disciples of the Incarnation should pray?

Practicing Advent Joy

Whenever you are in need of divine help, pray as a true believer, "Rise up, O God, from within me, so your liberating love will inspire me to be free of all obstacles."

*As an Advent sojourner let my prayers awaken me
to the power of your presence within me.*

Experiencing Advent at the intersection of Broadway and Bethlehem isn't frustrating but grace-filled. One of the graces of Advent can be found by transforming the familiar slogan "Put Christ back in Christmas" into "Put Christmas back in Christmas!" Instead of being swept away by the season's tsunami of "buy, buy, buy," or drowning in all the season's "shoulds," strive to give yourself a classic, graceful Christmas.

Enjoy the graces of sending Christmas greetings as sacraments of communion with your old friends. Rejoice in the grace of putting flesh on your love by giving gifts to your blood family and to your incarnational family—the needy and lonely. Let the marketplace's ubiquitous holiday music be a graced reminder of your discipleship in the never-ending cycle of God becoming incarnate in the world, including the secular merchandizing of the birth of Christ. That statement of God's enfleshment in the unseemly hustle and bustle of pre-Christmas shopping may be shocking to some. What is truly shocking is the Incarnation! God doesn't dwell within us in some disembodied spiritual realm, but has taken on human flesh in Jesus and in us—warts and all. Now that is scandalously shocking!

Practicing Advent Joy

Watch steadily this day for the grace of Emmanuel, God-with-us, in every task and quiet moment, in every bauble, twinkling light, and ringing carol.

I rejoice, O God, that you never act half-heartedly
but have taken on flesh in all you have created.

Second Sunday of Advent

To live Advent joyously in the spirit of Broadway or a shopping mall decorated for Christmas seems contrary to this season's somber theology and austere worship. Since the thirteenth century Advent has had a tone of repentance echoed in the cry of John the Baptist: "Reform your lives; God's reign is at hand." Advent spirituality has been shaped by calls for conversion and the dire warning of the end times that we heard about on the first Sunday of Advent. Yet, we don't live in the thirteenth century but in the twenty-first! We need a new theological spirituality suited for the Advent of today's world.

A principle of liberation theology is that theological reflections should arise out of a conversation with what is happening in the world where people live. What is happening in our world is that Christmas has already come! We can't ignore that reality, so instead of trying to live in an artificial Advent world, let's have a conversation with the all-pervasive festivity of Christmas.

Practicing Advent Joy

So ask your Christmas decorations, "How do you remind me of God's enfleshment in Jesus and in the world?" And while writing your greeting cards, ask them, "Can this, my holy homework, make for me a more joyous, more blessed Christmas than the one that Broadway offers?"

Oh every old carol I hear, increase my Advent longing.
Oh Christmas everywhere, sharpen my anticipation and watchful Christian eyes!

Since time began, subjugated peoples have sung of their longing for a liberator to come and topple their despised overlords. Our Hebrew ancestors yeaned for an Emmanuel, for a Messiah. This Anointed One symbolized for them the coming of a Messianic Age, a Godly time of freedom from debts, hunger, and violence. Jesus declared that this Age of God had arrived and called it "the Kingdom of God." The work of his disciples was to bring it to completeness, and he had them pray, "Thy Kingdom come, thy will be done."

Jesus taught that just as every birth is a gift, so the Kingdom is a gift from heaven. It is God who is birthing this New Divine Era, and we are to be dutiful midwives attending this blessed event. By being its midwives we are incorporated into God's way of living, and that kind of living brings to flower this New Era of non-violence, equality, and abundance for all. C. S. Lewis said that whenever we pray, "Thy will be done," God whispers back, "No, rather your will be done!" With all my heart I must will the existence of the Kingdom, and by my actions help it appear. Our will is to be God's will.

Practicing Advent Joy

Daily you stand at a hundred crossroads: to be kind or rude, stingy or generous, peaceful or angry. Choose so that your every choice is God's choice, and so make each day into a Christmas—a holy birth of Christ.

God of endless love,
Be my choice split-second or calculated, may I choose
Christmas, with my will one with yours, so Love can be
birthed again today.

Second Tuesday of Advent

Along with last Tuesday's prayer of Pierre Teilhard de Chardin, another excellent Advent prayer is one by King Solomon that easily could have been on the lips of Mary of Nazareth. God said to wise Solomon, "Ask for whatever you wish, and it will be granted to you." Being wise, King Solomon—whose name is derived from *shalom,* which means "peace"—didn't ask for the wealth of gold and treasures but for what could make him truly rich. His prayer response to God was, "O Lord, give your servant a hearing heart" (1 Kings 3:5, 9).

Because Mary possessed a hearing heart, she heard God's rich invitation to her in the angel's seemingly impossible message. Your marriage or personal relationships can be made much richer if you acquire the gift of a hearing heart, one capable of truly listening.

Practicing Advent Joy

Pray for a hearing heart. Discipline yourself to truly listen to others. With a hearing heart you can understand the unspoken messages in the daily commotion of family life, and also perceive in the diverse noisy tongues of the marketplace the sounds of God's voice.

God of whispers and shouts of joy,
Unclog my heart stuffed with me and my struggles
so it can become a listening, hearing, Advent heart.

Sometimes religion seems to have condemned our society as secular and urges us to take God to our workplace, the classroom, and the marketplace. This view of anti-Incarnation theology sees the world as the domain of the devil and requires that objects within it be blessed to rescue them from the devil's grip. So before they are used, rosaries, even crosses, are blessed, as are Advent wreaths and Christmas trees. But an awakened Advent sojourner knows God already abides in the workplace and that our Advent wreaths don't need to be blessed. What needs blessing is we ourselves!

Blessings should be worded to open our eyes to see and enjoy the presence of God in all of life's good things. Advent then can be experienced as a four-week eye-opening blessing to help us find God abiding in a deeply energizing way in all things. Then Advent is an adventure of discovery in which no stone is left unturned in uncovering the divine mystery. Such adventure requires unwavering faith in the Christmas Marvel of Marvels: God's choice to abide with and in us!

Practicing Advent Joy

Give an Advent cry of joy each time you find God in some new and previously undiscovered place or event, and even more breathtaking, some unanticipated person!

Gracious God,
open my eyes and heart and mind on this Advent treasure hunt,
as I go looking for you hidden in the most unlikely of places and
improbable persons.

Second Thursday of Advent

A good Advent should include throwing away your creed! Your creed causes you to discredit your personal experiences of God in the mundane. The one to which I refer isn't the Apostles' Creed, but the "Ain't-worthy Creed"! This negative creed begins:

> I believe that ordinary people, being insignificant,
> are unsuited for mystical experiences.
> I believe those not schooled in theology and scripture
> are not equipped for supernatural experiences.
> I believe that divine visitations happen only to saints.

Throw that creed into the garbage disposal! To feel the nearness of God in another person or an everyday event is to have a mystical experience. Don't be blinded by the fact that yours are not spectacular like those in Hollywood films and lack rumbling thunder and blinding lights!

Here is an Advent secret: The mundane is drenched with the Divine! For divine encounters, use Bethlehem as your compass. The cowshed birth of Jesus, unlike Mount Sinai, had no fear-instilling thunder and flashing fire, yet God was present.

Practicing Advent Joy

Whenever you have an intense sense of the Presence of God in the midst of some human activity or mundane place, don't dismiss it as an illusion. Reverence it. Be grateful that for you the thin veil that separates this world from the other was briefly lifted.

Lord God,
Help me remember that just as easily as I can turn a sweater
inside out, we believers can experience the sacred inner world.

Some view a "pure" Advent, devoid of Christmas decorations and music, as a religious ideal. In the real world such a purified Advent is possible only within a cloistered convent or monastery. And even there, a stern superior is required to ensure that no Christmas virus invades the pure Advent environment. Parishes and private homes also strive in Advent to maintain Christmas-free environments to ensure there is no separation from Christ. Yet St. Paul asks, "What can separate us from the love of Christ?" And he answers, "Nothing!"

To Paul's long list of what can't separate us, including persecutions and tribulations, add decorating your home for Christmas, gift shopping, baking cookies, and enjoying Christmas parties. Those who fear that without a pure Advent their Christmas will be ruined should ponder the Chinese proverb, "Two-thirds of what you see is behind your eyes." If you find it difficult or impossible to be connected to Christ in Broadway's yuletide decorations or Christmas TV commercials, take a few minutes now to look behind your eyes. Behind our eyes reside our unconscious beliefs.

Practicing Advent Joy

Today's Advent assignment is to adopt the Creed of the Incarnation. Then wholeheartedly believe in Christmas, that God became enfleshed in Jesus, in you, and in the world. Live this creed, and nothing in this world can separate you from Christ.

Using eyes of faith to see you, O God, enmeshed in Christmas-come-early,
I also can see you in aliens, strangers, and those I dislike.

Second Saturday of Advent

Tomorrow, unless you live in a cloistered convent or a monastery, you will depart from one world to enter another—the purple world of Advent. As you enter the church vestibule of the Advent world, don't wipe your shoes clean of the untidy world in which you've lived these past six days—take all of it inside with you. Don't empty your pockets of all the unseemly stuff of your world where you work and live, as if passing through an airport security gate, but carry it all with you into church. Your Sunday worship will be made richer by your encounters with the Holy One in the tinsel and holly-adorned marketplace, and by the touches of God you've felt in the shoving crowds of shoppers.

Imagine yourself contagious with these worldly divine exchanges so your secular nitty-gritty God virus can infect those with whom you worship. At the offertory symbolically drop into the collection basket your holiday discoveries, more precious than gold, of the Divine Presence. Then go to Holy Communion with a heart made worthy by your love labors of writing Christmas cards, shopping for gifts, and decorating your home for Christmas.

Practicing Advent Joy

As Mass ends tomorrow, depart as a citizen of both worlds, rejoicing that God dwells equally in both! Depart the Advent world into the wider world, eager and energized to find God in even more and unlikely places.

O Come, God-Made-Flesh, and reveal yourself to me
in the ten thousand different Bethlehems of my world.

Third Sunday of Advent

Christmas was first celebrated in Rome in the middle of the fourth century, and in the next century Advent appeared as two weeks of joyful festivity echoing Paul's call to "rejoice always." Today the old Roman spirit of Advent joy returns, and the gospel speaks of John the Baptist. Elijah was expected to return before the arrival of the Messiah, and many saw John as a reincarnated Elijah. He denied it, saying he was only a voice in the desert preparing the way for the Messiah.

We believe Jesus fulfilled John's prophecy, but the Messianic Age he began hasn't yet fully come. Jesus was the Prince of Peace—or nonviolence, a far more descriptive word for peace. He taught that we sow the seeds of tomorrow by the way we respond today to others as individual persons and as one nation to another. If today you sow words or deeds of violence, tomorrow you reap a harvest ripe with violence, as today's world reveals all too clearly. If the peaceable Messianic Age is to fully emerge, we must be its prophets, and true prophets are living enfleshments of what they prophesize. As Messianic Age prophets, by our nonviolent words and behavior we make God tangible to others.

Practicing Advent Joy

Your vocation is far more demanding than was Ascetic John's: to proclaim by your joyful nonviolence not the *future* coming of Emmanuel but that *God among us* has already arrived!

O God of Joy,
Help me to clearly announce the peace of Emmanuel
by my gentle nonviolence in word and deed
even in the holiday hustle and bustle.

Nativity crèches are compelling liturgical shrines to small children. I retain some charming childhood memories of kneeling with my two little brothers before our family's simple crib set as my mother led us in a nine-day Christmas novena. This brief, simple novena—a holy counter of the days until Christmas—fused together as one the coming of Christ's birth and the coming of Santa Claus for me. Later in life, I learned that the Hindus in India also have novenas. Prior to certain festivals of their gods they celebrate nine days of dancing and singing the praises of God. Dancing is the global sign of joy, and the more joyful any feast is, the more it should be anticipated with joy— even with fun.

Having fun and praying are often judged incompatible; yet isn't fun only an amusing aspect of joy? To have fun doesn't rob anyone of the spirit of the approaching feast of Christmas, but rather having fun enhances the true spirit of the feast. In a gloomy world sadly lacking joy, having fun may be the best of all prayers to prepare for the birth of Joy Incarnate.

Practicing Advent Joy

Consider beginning your own family—or personal, if you live alone—Christmas novena on the sixteenth of December. As you create your homemade novena, be inspired by the delightful dancing of Hindu novenas, and make yours one of fun and joyful anticipation.

Christmas commemorates the birth of Joy Unquenchable; may I prepare for it with fun and a playful, dancing spirit.

The Messianic legend included the belief that the prophet Elijah would return before the arrival of the Messiah and his age of justice and nonviolence—a belief recorded several times in the gospels. Eight hundred years had passed since Elijah had died and was taken up to heaven in a fiery chariot, when Joseph and his pregnant wife Mary traveled to Bethlehem. Jesus was thought by some to be a reincarnated Elijah. He denied it and creatively enlivened the legend, saying of John the Baptist, "He is Elijah, the one who is to come!" Was he was correct, or did he know that every age needs the return of the prophetic spirit of Elijah?

What the world needs to be reborn isn't the return of some long-dead prophet but the appearance of energetic, zealous prophets as living "God-among-us-Emmanuels." God chooses prophets, but no one wishes to be so chosen. Yet in Baptism each of us was anointed with chrism as a royal, priestly, and prophetic person. For the Age of Emmanuel to bloom, a whole crowd of prophetic people is needed—not the arrival of just one or two great prophets.

Practicing Advent Joy

The trumpet of Advent calls us to take up our duties as baptism-anointed prophets. Speak up for peace so that the Messianic Age of love and nonviolence begun two thousand years ago in Bethlehem may become visible through you today.

O Emmanuel,
I wait for no return of Elijah. Release his spirit within me
so the peaceable Kingdom of God becomes visible on earth.

Delightfully decorated evergreen trees and melodic old Christmas carols make for a beautiful Christmas, but what would make it even more beautiful is for Elijah to appear. Not a reincarnation of that old, dead prophet, but for his visionary spirit to appear in each of us. The Advent season began with a Lenten-like call to do penance and confess our sins, yet we best prepare for an Incarnational Christmas by becoming prophets!

"That's impossible," we say, yet John the Baptist gave some easily accomplishable guidelines for how you can prophesize: "Let the one with two coats give one to a person with none. Share your food with the needy. In business be just, not greedy. Do not bully anyone. Falsely denounce no one, and be contented."

Anyone can perform these prophetic deeds, sharing with others what you have, be it clothing, food, money, or your most precious gift—your time. Love of neighbor is often merely intellectual. The radical revolutionary prophets of our times are those content with what they have, and who then share some of it with those in need.

Practicing Advent Joy

The seductive advertisements of this holiday season increase our appetites for more and more, so become prophetic by being contented with what you already have, and then, in the realistic and practical love of Christ, share some of that with those in need.

Holy Child of Bethlehem,
Challenge me to do the works of a prophet that I can perform:
finding contentment and loving concretely by sharing with others.

THIRD THURSDAY OF ADVENT

Another name for prophets is visionaries. The prophets of our time are those who can envision a Christmas of a God-enfleshed world and see themselves doing good things. St. Theresa of Avila was such a visionary prophet who said, "Christ has no body on earth but ours, no hands but ours ... ours are the feet with which he goes about doing good." Travel guide Theresa shows us the way to Christmas: by using our bodies, our hands and feet, to do practical good deeds for others. While it sounds easy, it isn't, since we are so self-absorbed, acting like squabbling children greedily clinging to their toys.

The way to Bethlehem isn't a *broad* way, for as Jesus said, "The way is narrow." Being slender as a thread, we can easily fall off the narrow way of Jesus by being engrossed in the unimportant details of life, especially in this holiday season. Greed is a crippling, heart-cramping virus contracted at our earliest age that fills our streets with misdirected souls. The well-trodden path of those who think only about themselves and of acquiring more and more is indeed broad and crowded. But rejoice, for Christmas is the antidote, offering healing in countless opportunities to be big-hearted.

Practicing Advent Joy

So travel to Christmas on the Narrow Way, the pathway of the nonviolent meek, and the royal highway taken by those who dare to be generous beyond their budgets. Remember the Salvation Army bell ringers, your local food bank, and parish giving-tree. Do for others what they cannot.

Divine is the healing therapy of generosity and kindness;
it uncurls a greedy tightened fist and expands a small heart.

THIRD FRIDAY OF ADVENT

Advent is a time for not only works of mercy and justice but also prayer, for which Elijah is a good guide. In these busy days preparing for Christmas it is difficult to find time for prayer, but being busy is all the more reason to steal time for the prayer of Elijah. Having incurred the wrath of Queen Jezebel, he feared for his life and ran away into the wilderness. There he sought God in the expected ways: a scorching fire, a howling hurricane, and an earthquake. But God wasn't in any of them. Sitting in his hideout cave he was left with deafening silence, and in the midst of that silence he heard God in a soft whisper, "Elijah, what are you doing here?"

Christmas is almost here, and with so many things left to do we go rushing about busily trying to accomplish them, even the doing of good. Once aware you're too busy, become a thief and steal time from the clock to imitate Elijah. Improvise your own cave—any quiet place will do—and then patiently wait in silence. If you can do this, God will also challenge you in a soft whisper: "Dear one, what are you doing rushing about?"

Practicing Advent Joy

When irritated from being too busy and rushing everywhere causes you to angrily lash out at some clerk or a family member, pause so God can whisper, "Dear one, why are you so awfully busy?"

Ancient Prophet Elijah,
help me put on the brakes and stop my rushing
so by slowing down I can be lovingly more patient and kind.

Third Saturday of Advent

The long shadows of the Advent repentance of Elijah and John the Baptist still linger over our joyful anticipation of Christmas. Repentance implies contrition and going to confession (that once was required to go to Communion on Christmas), but repentance has another meaning. It also means to be renewed, to be a new and better person, like the real you instead of only a Xerox copy of others. As victims of saturation advertising and a great need for acceptance, we so often feel coerced to dress as look-alike duplications of others. Sadly, we also pattern our values, thinking, and behavior on what is socially acceptable instead of using the unique pattern given us by Jesus.

Advent is preparation time for the birth of Jesus, and also for your own new birth! Seriously consider being reborn, which Jesus said was a necessity for life in the Kingdom. In these few days before Christmas, go into labor with God's Spirit as your midwife and begin to give birth to the person you always wanted to be. You are far more than made in God's image; you are an enfleshment of God in this world.

Practicing Advent Joy

Begin today, your birthday on Christmas, by becoming a new, authentic you—a Christ-bearer—the loving, living presence of God.

Along with the shepherds, may I attend a holy birth,
my own re-birth in the New Bethlehem where I live each day.

Today's patron of belief is Mary of Nazareth, for she trusted the angel's message that by God's Spirit she was with child—chosen by God to give birth to Emmanuel. As Christians, we believe many things, like those proclaimed in the Creed. And some of what we are asked to believe is seemingly unbelievable. The reflections of this Advent have challenged you to believe that the same Holy Spirit who brought God to human birth through Mary's body has done the same for you and for others!

Do you believe God is actually enfleshed in your body, or did that happen only for Jesus? If because you are so ordinary you are tempted to doubt that for you such a divine marvel is possible, look at your Christmas nativity set. Notice who is represented as being there, or rather who isn't: There are no figures representing Jerusalem's wealthy elite, its temple priests, and learned scribes! Those who are represented are the very lowest members of Jewish society, poor illiterate shepherds invited by God's angelic messengers. Look closely at the shepherds—they represent you and all of us who are so insignificant in the eyes of the world. Christmas crèches and the gospel of Bethlehem validate the truth that God's Presence is to be found in the most unexpected places and most unlikely persons.

Practicing Advent Joy

Look at your nativity set and dare to believe.

As Mary trusted in God's unbelievable indwelling in her, may I also dare to believe the same marvel is true for me.

Fourth Monday of Advent

These days just before Christmas are crammed with graces and offer opportunities for celebrating the pre-biblical sacrament of hospitality as you welcome family and friends into your home. Hospitality in Hebrew literally means "love of a stranger." Blessed are these pre-Christmas days when our hearts are more than ever inclined not only to welcome those we know and love, but also to be kind to those in need. Look not on your acts of generosity as charity, but as offering hospitality to those who need what you can give. Every gift given to someone in need is a wondrous gift exchange of hospitality between you and the Risen Christ. The gift of love you receive in return is immensely superior to that which you gave.

These last days of Advent are abundantly rich in opportunities to express love to your family and show hospitality (love) to the stranger. As they approached Bethlehem, the young father, Joseph, and his pregnant wife, Mary, hungered for a loving welcome, a warm meal, and a safe place to stay. As old inhospitable Bethlehem created in Mother Mary a hunger for hospitality, may these days make you hunger for hospitality, but not to receive it so much as to give it.

Practicing Advent Joy

Be ravenously hungry in your desire to extend with smiling eyes your hospitable love to strangers on the street, and do the same to those you greet at your front door.

By my smile and sincere holiday greetings to strangers
may I greet with loving hospitality my disguised Lover.

Fourth Tuesday of Advent

These nights before Christmas are the longest and darkest of the year. Luke's Gospel gives voice to the ancient yearning for the return of the light and an end to this deadly darkness: "Then the Daybreak from on high will visit us." Daybreak is a code word for Messiah, whose arrival in the darkly shrouded world would be like ten thousand suns exploding. Like previous ages, our age longs for that divine Daybreak to banish the darkness of hate, greed, and violence. Because of the "tender mercies of our God," we trust that this dawn will come.

Insurance companies once referred to disastrous storms as acts of God, but if you desire to see acts of God, look not at natural disasters but at Jesus in whom God was enfleshed. His behavior was Godlike in its mercy, and so he called his disciples to "be merciful, even as God is merciful." Earth's ancient, never-ending, diabolic dark night of discrimination, violence, and war will end only when the Daybreak appears in our acts of mercy.

Practicing Advent Joy

Be merciful—making your love practical (hands-on), being tenderly compassionate, and authentically kind. Then your year will be transformed into 365 Christmas days of God's mercy.

God of mercy,
Do not let me long lament the world's evil darkness;
teach me to become Daybreak, happily dispelling darkness.

A nativity crèche isn't another Christmas decoration; it is a shrine rich in mystical insights into the Incarnation. Look lovingly at your crèche and see Mary, Joseph, and the holy infant. See the shepherds and their sheep, a cow and donkey, and in some, the shepherds' shaggy dog. In the great Christmas story these animal figures are not bit actors; they're prophets of the incarnation. Pierre Teilhard de Chardin in his *Hymn to the Universe* said, "Through your own incarnation, my God, all matter is henceforth incarnate." The animals of the crèche symbolize all creatures in which God is enfleshed—not only in humans, but "all matter." To fully celebrate the breadth and depth of Christmas, open your eyes to God present in your dog or cat and the scarlet cardinal perched on an evergreen branch. Your pet and those of others are not dumb animals; rather they and all creatures are living presences of the Divine Mystery.

True disciples express their faith in all that the mystery of Christmas represents by the way they relate to animals. The shepherds believed and saw God in the infant lying in the animal feed trough in the dirty straw and the entire stable shimmering with God's glory.

Practicing Advent Joy

Pray for the gift of shepherds' eyes to see your crèche not as a charming replication of that first Christmas, but as a holy window into how unbelievably inclusive was God's incarnation!

Joy to the world, let heaven and nature sing,
for all of nature shares in God's incarnation.

Fourth Thursday of Advent

(For Christmas Eve, see the next reflection)

In family nativity scenes it is often the custom to telescope the arrival of the Magi Kings by placing them a short distance behind the shepherds. These wise men from the Orient were not Jews and didn't believe in the God of Joseph and Mary. Their presence at our Christmas shrines is essential since they are included in the gospel story and because they symbolize the global reach of the mystery of the incarnation. The Magi embody God's enfleshment in those who belong to the great religions of the world and those nonbelievers whom the Holy Spirit inspires to become God-seekers. The classic Christmas carol, "O Come, All Ye Faithful," creates an image of the Magi kneeling in faithful adoration in front of God enfleshed in the infant. The call *Venite, Adoremus,* "come let us adore," comes to us also. Dismiss any thoughts of God being unreachable and remote from your daily world, for the Divine Mystery without exception has penetrated all created things.

Practicing Advent Joy

"Adore" comes from the Latin, "ad," in front of, and "ora," to pray. As the curtain begins to rise on Christmas, express what you believe by adoration, like the Magi did. Stand in front of everything in the world and pray in wonder.

O come, all ye faithful believers of what is unbelievable,
that along with Jesus, your flesh, your very being, is God-filled.

The goals of Advent and of the spiritual life are identical: to become aware that you and God are one. Jesus announced he had achieved that goal when he said, "The Father and I are one." Today, Christmas Eve, concludes our Advent preparation for Christmas, the feast of God becoming incarnate in Jesus, in each of us, and in all creation. To accept this astonishing indwelling in yourself requires the same strength of faith demanded of the shepherds and the Magi. They saw only a newborn infant cradled in the poorest of places yet believed he was divine — the promised Messiah. More than being temples of the Holy Spirit, Jesus and each of us are the living presence of God in our world! St. Ignatius of Loyola expressed this shockingly sacred reality by using the metaphor of the sun for God and the rays of the sun for us humans. Just as it is impossible to look and separate the blazing sun from its rays, so the same is true for God and us.

Practicing Advent Joy

Tomorrow is Christmas, the birth of the Daybreak from on high. Contemplate the mystery of yourself fused as one with God. See yourself as a living, luminous ray of Divine Light.

O Daystar of Bethlehem, remove my eclipse of doubt
so I may radiate your light into every corner of my life.

Finally, we have arrived at Christmas, the great feast of gift giving. Each year all the lavish Christmas decorations of Broadway and Main Street lure us in to buy our presents, and the quiet mystery of Bethlehem lures us in to the heart of a different kind of present. The noun "present" originated from the old French for "bringing something into someone's presence." Every Christmas celebrates that first Christmas in Bethlehem and the gift given Jesus of God being *present* in him, filling every cell of his flesh. I hope these weeks of Advent reflections have prepared you to see among your gifts on this Christmas Day one truly magnificent gift, one beyond calculation—God *present* in you!

Your gift is beautifully wrapped in your human flesh. The most excellent way you can express gratitude to the Gift Giver is by being joyful about your gift and never growing tired of it.

Practicing Advent Joy

Give thanks then for the rest of your life, as did Jesus, joyfully wearing your gift on the outside so everyone who encounters you will have a tangible experience of the living God.

Joy to the world, the Word is made flesh,
at Broadway and at Bethlehem—
in the already here of God's reign
and in the still-awaited fullness of its promise.
Joy to my world, for God is enfleshed in me!

Edward Hays is the co-founder and a moving spirit of Forest of Peace Publishing. He is the author of over thirty best-selling books on contemporary spirituality. Many bear his own art. He has also served as director of Shantivanam, a Midwest center for contemplative prayer, and as a chaplain of the state penitentiary in Lansing, Kansas. He has spent extended periods on pilgrimage in the Near East, the Holy Land, and India. He continues his ministry as a prolific writer and painter.